Life Stories
Mother Teresa

Wayne Jackman

Illustrated by Peter Dennis
Wayland

Life Stories

Louis Braille
Christopher Columbus
Anne Frank
Gandhi
Helen Keller
Martin Luther King
Florence Nightingale
Mother Teresa

Cover and frontispiece *Mother Teresa in the simple white and blue sari she always wears.*

Series editor: Anna Girling
Consultant: Nigel Smith
Designer: Loraine Hayes

First published in 1993 by
Wayland (Publishers) Ltd
61 Western Road, Hove
East Sussex BN3 1JD, England

British Library Cataloguing in Publication Data
Jackman, Wayne
Mother Teresa. – (Life Stories Series)
I. Title   II. Series
266.2092
ISBN 0 7502 0725 6

Typeset by Dorchester Typesetting Group Ltd
Printed in Italy by G. Canale & C.S.p.A., Turin
Bound in Belgium by Casterman S.A.

Contents

Words printed in **bold** appear in the glossary.

The early years

On a hot day in a small town in eastern Europe, a shopkeeper named Nikola Bojaxhiu was anxiously awaiting the birth of his third child. The date was 27 August 1910 and the town was Skopje in **Macedonia**. Suddenly a small cry was heard. 'Your wife, Dronda, has had a baby girl,' he was told. They named the baby Agnes.

Little did they realize that years later she was to become Mother Teresa, the best-known **missionary** in the world!

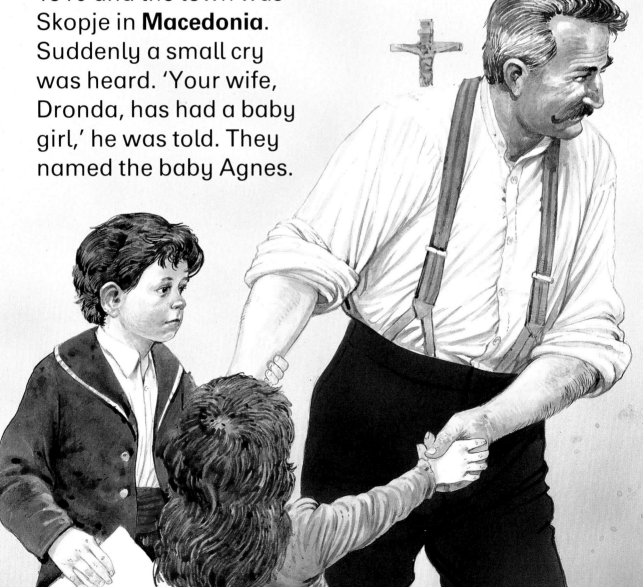

Baby Agnes grew up to become Mother Teresa, the best-known missionary in the world.

5

The small town of Skopje, where Agnes was born.

Like many of their neighbours, the Bojaxhiu family were devout **Roman Catholics**. Agnes grew up with her sister Aga and her brother Lazar in a house full of love and happiness. Although her father died when Agnes was still young, she remembers her childhood as being always 'exceptionally happy'.

As a girl, Agnes took a keen interest in stories about missionaries helping the poor in India. She began to think that God had some special work for her to do in India, so she decided to become a missionary **nun**. It was a brave decision because it meant that she was giving up the chance of marriage and a family of her own.

Sister Teresa

In 1928, when she was only eighteen, Agnes joined the missionary **order** of Loreto nuns. She was sent to their **convent** in Ireland to begin her training to become a nun. Imagine how hard it must have been to be so far from home. After a few months in Ireland, Agnes was sent to the Loreto convent in Darjeeling in India, where the rolling hills reminded her of her homeland. In 1931, Agnes took her first **vows** as a nun and chose the name Sister Teresa.

She was then sent to Calcutta to teach in the convent school, where many of the pupils were from wealthy homes.

7

Calcutta in the 1930s was a busy place.

In 1937, Sister Teresa became principal of the school. Though she knew teaching was useful work, the sights, smells and cries of poor people living in the **slums** outside the convent walls greatly upset her, and she wanted to help them.

Whenever she could, Sister Teresa would wander among the people of the slums, taking small gifts of food or medicines. When she had nothing to give, she simply offered words of comfort. Many people felt better just by looking at her kindly face.

9

A message from God

On 10 September 1946, Sister Teresa was travelling by train to Darjeeling for a brief rest. Suddenly she thought she heard the voice of God talking to her. She described it as 'hearing the call to give up all and follow Him (God) into the slums to serve Him among the poorest of the poor'. This was her '**Day of Inspiration**' and it is celebrated every year by her followers.

Sister Teresa chose to live among the very poor people of Calcutta.

Sister Teresa now knew exactly why God had brought her to India. She knew she must abandon her safe, easy life in the convent to go and live with the poor. She would eat the same food as they did; she would share their poverty and pain; she would comfort and care for them.

The white sari

Sister Teresa returned to the convent in Calcutta and immediately asked if she could leave to live and work as a nun in the slums. Permission was not given right away because working alone in the streets was considered far too dangerous. Sister Teresa waited patiently.

Her white and blue sari made Sister Teresa instantly recognizable.

A slum area in an Indian city.

She had faith that if God wanted her to work among the 'poorest of the poor', it would happen.

Two years later, in 1948, the **Pope** gave his blessing to her plans. Realizing that she would need medical skills, Sister Teresa spent several months training as a nurse. Then, with just 5 rupees (about 30 pence) in her pocket, she walked out into the slums of Calcutta.

Sister Teresa gave up her dark **nun's habit** and dressed like a poor Indian woman. She wore a simple white **sari** with blue lines along the edge. She pinned a small **crucifix** to her left shoulder. She has continued to dress in this way ever since.

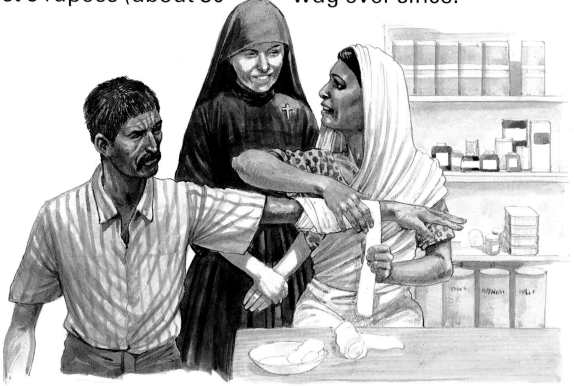

Sister Teresa's helpers give out food to the hungry.

Her work began with a school for the people living in the slums. In the open air, between the shacks, she used the dusty ground as a blackboard and a stick as her chalk. When people heard what she was doing, they sent gifts for her school. Next she started a **dispensary**, handing out medicines, bandages and food given to her by people who wanted to help. News of her work soon spread among the slums of Calcutta, and more and more people came to Sister Teresa looking for help.

15

The Missionaries of Charity

Sister Teresa soon had many willing helpers. They were mostly girls she had taught at the convent school. They wanted to follow her example and give up their comfortable homes to live and work among the poor in the dirty, smelly alleyways of Calcutta.

The Pope was so impressed with the work of Sister Teresa and her helpers that in 1950 he gave her permission to start a new order of nuns. She called her order The Congregation of the Missionaries of Charity and, as its leader, Sister Teresa became Mother Teresa. She set up the **Motherhouse**, the order's

Many poor people in Calcutta were dying in the streets.

headquarters, at 54a Lower Circular Road, Calcutta.

One day Mother Teresa stumbled over a dying woman lying outside a hospital. She carried the woman into the hospital, only to be told she was too poor and too ill to be treated.

But Mother Teresa refused to leave until the woman was cared for. After this happened, Mother Teresa knew she must find a home where poor people could die peacefully.

Within three days she had started her home. She called it Nirmal Hriday, which means Place of the Pure Hearts.

Many young girls joined Mother Teresa in caring for the sick.

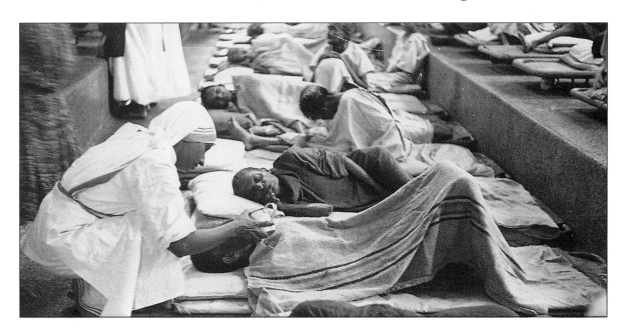

However, some **Hindu** priests were afraid that Mother Teresa and her nuns wanted to steal the dying people away from the Hindu religion. The priests tried to drive the nuns away; they even threw stones at the home. But when Mother Teresa took a dying Hindu priest into Nirmal Hriday and cared for him with loving kindness, they realized that people of all religions were treated the same at Nirmal Hriday.

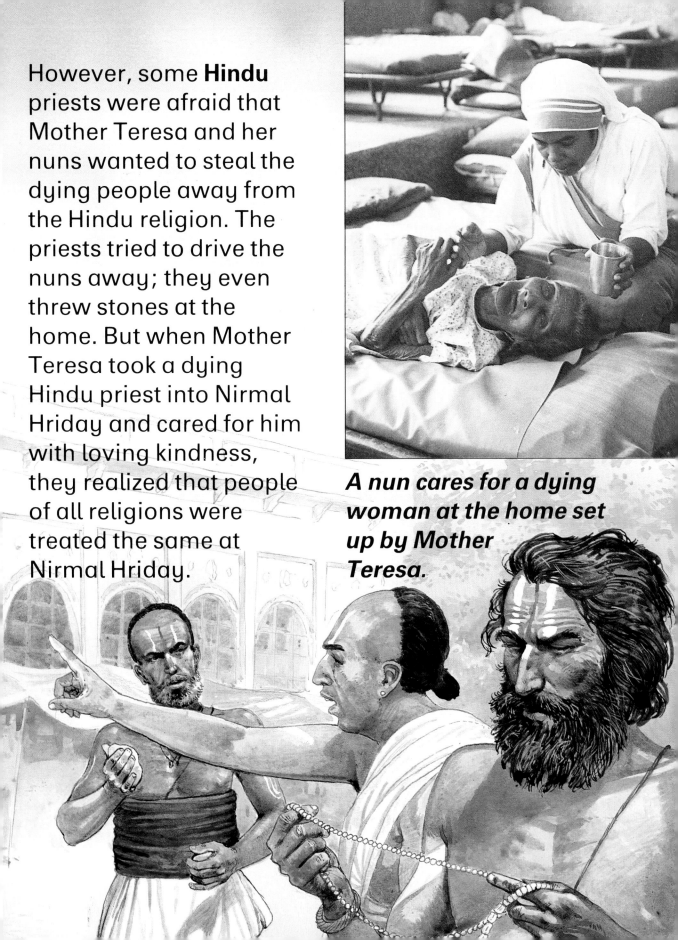

A nun cares for a dying woman at the home set up by Mother Teresa.

Mother Teresa is especially fond of little children. The streets of Calcutta are full of children needing help. Some are orphans, some are ill, and others have been abandoned by their parents who are too poor to look after them.

So Mother Teresa decided to start another special home, this time for children. She called it Shishu Bhavan (The Children's Home). The children she took in were often filthy and covered in **lice** and sores. However, Mother Teresa

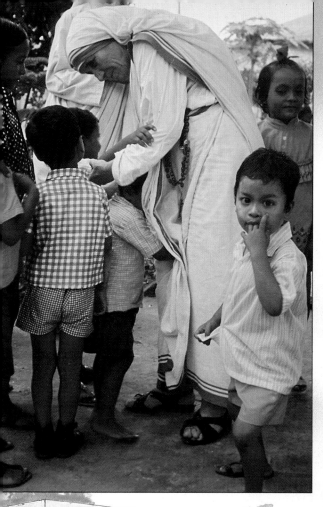

and her nuns nursed the children back to health and, whenever possible, found new, loving homes for them.

Another group who desperately needed help were the **lepers**. Lepers suffer from a terrible disease called leprosy.

Mother Teresa has a special fondness for children.

This deforms their bodies. Most people avoid any contact with lepers because they are afraid that they will catch the disease. But Mother Teresa has never been afraid. She would gladly wash and clean the lepers, loving them as much as any healthy person. In 1969 she started a leper village and called it Shanti Nagar (The Place of Peace).

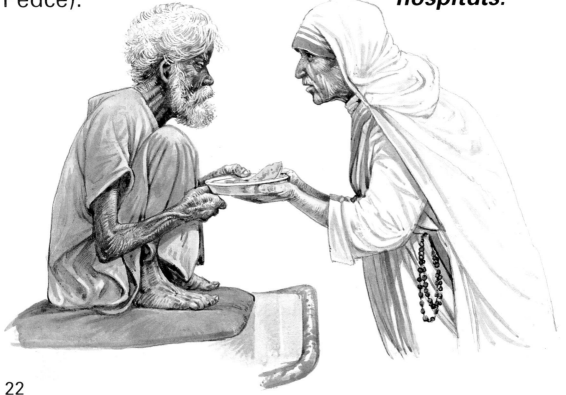

People queue for medicines at one of Mother Teresa's leprosy hospitals.

A harsh life

Mother Teresa and her nuns live an extremely harsh life. Each of them possesses only two saris, a crucifix, sandals and a prayer book.

The nuns' day begins at 4.30 am with prayers and **Mass**, followed by a simple breakfast. Then, before most of us are awake, they are already on their way to help the poor and needy.

Mother Teresa and her nuns always start the day with prayers.

The nuns work hard, handing out medicines.

Some of the sisters work in the home for the dying, some go to the leper village, some look after the children or teach in the schools. Other sisters walk through the streets handing out food.

Mother Teresa does the same work as the other sisters; she even takes her turn to clean the toilets. Often she works all day, not even stopping for a glass of water. She is always thinking of new ways to help the poor, never thinking of herself. Once, after a meal on an aeroplane, Mother Teresa asked all the passengers to collect their leftovers for her so that she could hand them out to the poor!

Mother Teresa often works from early morning to late at night, without a rest.

Mother Teresa says: 'The joy of helping the needy is reward enough.'

Mother Teresa and her Missionaries of Charity ask for nothing in return for all their hard work. For them the joy of helping the needy is reward enough. Mother Teresa has said: 'We are not forced to be happy; we are naturally happy because we have found what we have looked for.' She means that they are happy because they are doing God's work. In her own words, they are doing 'something beautiful for God'.

The world says thank you

Mother Teresa calls the people of the world 'my people', and her work has spread out from Calcutta to every corner of the world. Her missionaries have set up homes in poor countries such as Yemen and Ethiopia as well as in richer countries such as Australia and Britain.

Nuns now work around the world. This is Mother Teresa visiting Ethiopia.

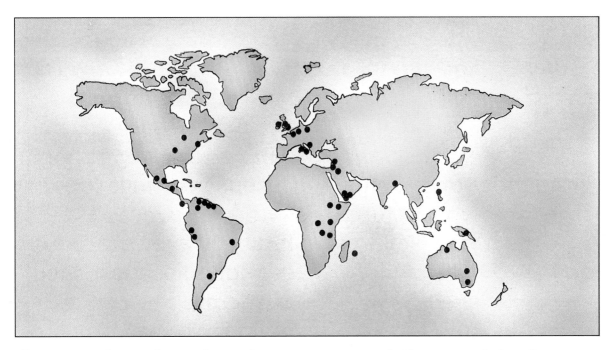

A map showing the places around the world where Mother Teresa's homes have been set up.

But how does this work get paid for? Rather than use up effort on asking governments for money, Mother Teresa prefers to trust in God. 'God will provide,' she says. Certainly there are thousands of well-wishers throughout the world who do give money.

Mother Teresa receiving the Nobel Peace Prize.

Perhaps the greatest honour Mother Teresa has received has been the **Nobel Peace Prize**, which was given to her in 1979. She used the prize money of almost £100,000 to bring further comfort to the poorest of the poor. Once again, Mother Teresa was able to do 'something beautiful for God'.

Date chart

1910 (27 August) Agnes Gouxha Bojaxhiu is born.

1928 Goes to the Loreto convent in Ireland and then to Darjeeling, India, to train as a nun.

1931 Takes her first vows and becomes Sister Teresa. Begins teaching at the convent school in Calcutta.

1937 Takes her final vows and becomes the principal of the convent school.

1946 (10 September) The 'Day of Inspiration'.

1948 Leaves the Loreto convent to work in the slums.

1950 Starts The Congregation of the Missionaries of Charity and becomes Mother Teresa.

1952 Opens Nirmal Hriday, a home for the dying.

1953 Opens Sishu Bhavan, a home for children.

1965 Given permission by the Pope to open houses for the poor outside India.

1969 Opens Shanti Nagar, a leper village.

1979 Receives the Nobel Peace Prize.

1985 Visits Ethiopia to help with famine problems.

1990s Suffers from various illnesses. 'Soon I think God will call me home,' she says.

Glossary

Convent The building where nuns live.

Crucifix A cross that represents the cross on which Jesus Christ died.

'Day of Inspiration' Inspiration means having a good idea. This was the day Mother Teresa decided to live and work with the poor and needy.

Dispensary A place where medicines are given out.

Hindu A follower of Hinduism, which is the main religion of India.

Lepers People who are suffering from the disease known as leprosy. Leprosy causes sores on the skin and disfigures the body.

Lice Insects that live on human hair and skin.

Macedonia An ancient country that for much of the twentieth century was part of Yugoslavia.

Mass A religious service in the Roman Catholic Church.

Missionary A person who is sent by the Christian church to another country to teach people there about Christianity.

Motherhouse The main headquarters of an order of nuns.

Nobel Peace Prize A prize given every year by the Nobel Foundation to someone who has helped to bring peace to the world.

Nun A woman who is a member of a religious order and spends her life serving God.

Nun's habit The clothes a nun wears. The Loreto habit was a black dress.

Order A particular group of nuns who live by a certain set of rules.

Pope The head of the Roman Catholic Church.

Roman Catholics Christians who belong to the Church that is headed by the Pope.

Sari A long piece of material that is wrapped around the body, worn by Indian women.

Slum A crowded part of a city that has flimsy, makeshift houses.

Vows Promises made to God. A nun promises to live unmarried, to own few things and to spend many hours praying.

Books to read

Heart of Joy by Mother Teresa (Fount Paperbacks, 1988)

Mother Teresa by Charlotte Gray (Wolfhound Press, 1988)

My Life with the Poor by Mother Teresa (Ballantine, 1987)

Useful addresses

UK
Co-workers of Mother Teresa, 6 Church Street, Old Woking, Surrey.

Australia
Missionary Sisters of Charity, 149 George Street, Fitzroy 3065, Melbourne.

USA
Missionary Sisters of Charity, 335 East 145th Street, New York 10451.

Index

Picture acknowledgements
The publishers would like to thank the following: Camera Press 12 top, 14, 16, 17, 21, 22, 23 both, 24 (all S.K. Dutt), cover and frontispiece (W. Bennett); Impact 11 (P. Cavendish), 12 bottom (B. Edwards); Mary Evans Picture Library 8; Rex Features 5 (The Times), 28 (Norks Press); Topham 19 (B. Walton), 26, 27; Zefa 6.